LED ZEPPELIN

TRIVIA BOOK

Uncover The Epic History With

Facts Every Fan Needs To Know!

By

Dale Raynes

ISBN: 978-1-955149-26-6

TABLE OF CONTENTS

LED ZEPPELIN

Starting as what appeared to be yet another English blues-rock band, from their first album, it was clear that Led Zeppelin was so much more than that. They took the platform of the blues-rock genre and built on it in several sophisticated directions, branching into folk and progressive rock without ever over-reaching or collapsing into a pomposity. Oh yeah, and they invented hard rock while they were at it. *And* they sold 300 million albums worldwide without ever selling out.

Led Zeppelin was quite simply one of the best and most influential rock bands of all time. Everything about them was larger than life. When asked by a reporter if all the rumors about their backstage behavior and debauchery were accurate, singer Robert Plant said, "It's all true. When we do something, we just do it bigger and better than anybody else. When there are no holds barred, there are no holds barred." Truer words have never been spoken.

CHAPTER I:

GROWING UP

1. Who is the youngest member of Led Zeppelin?
   a. Robert Plant
   b. Jimmy Page
   c. John Paul Jones
   d. John Bonham

2. In which London suburb was Jimmy Page born?
   a. Bexley
   b. Teddington
   c. Heston
   d. Chiswick

3. Where did Jimmy get his first guitar?
   a. He saved up for it and bought it.
   b. His parents bought him one.
   c. He stole it.
   d. It was around the house.

4. Like so many guitarists of his generation, Scotty Moore from Elvis's first band inspired Jimmy to start playing. Which song does Jimmy say got him to start playing?

   a. "Baby Let's Play House"

   b. "That's All Right Momma"

   c. "I'm Left, You're Right, She's Gone"

   d. "Milkcow Blues Boogie"

5. Jimmy brought his guitar with him to school. How did they react to his precocious talent?

   a. They let him play it on his breaks.

   b. They encouraged him to play in school events.

   c. They confiscated it.

   d. They expelled him for bringing it.

6. True or False: When Jimmy was 14, he appeared on Huw Wheldon's *All Your Own* talent quest and won.

7. While Led Zeppelin was a London band, Robert grew up in the Midlands. In which oddly named Midland town did he spend most of his childhood?

a. Halesowen

b. Mamble

c. Queen Camel

d. Picklescott

8. Why was Robert expelled from grammar school?

   a. He was caught smoking in the bathroom.

   b. His hair.

   c. He was always cutting class.

   d. Talking back to the teachers.

9. What did Robert study at college?

   a. Law

   b. History

   c. Philosophy

   d. Accounting

10. Robert is a serious soccer fan (though, of course, he would call it football). Which team has he supported since childhood?

    a. West Bromwich Albion FC

    b. Wolverhampton Wanderers FC

    c. Coventry City FC

    d. Aston Villa FC

11. At what age did Robert Plant move out of his parents' house?
    a. 15
    b. 16
    c. 17
    d. 18

12. In which of England's counties was John Paul Jones born?
    a. Kent
    b. Berkshire
    c. Kent
    d. Surrey

13. True or False: John Paul Jones played the first bass he bought at age 16 on the first Led Zeppelin albums.

14. True or False: Like most bassists, John Paul Jones first learned to play guitar and then switched to bass when he saw more demand.

15. True or False: John Paul Jones was named after the great American naval commander who excelled in the Revolutionary War.

16. How old was John Paul Jones when he joined his first band?
    a. 13
    b. 14
    c. 15
    d. 16

17. True or False: John Bonham's birth was so messy and complicated that it was declared a medical miracle that he survived.

18. When John brought back a report card from school, what did the headmaster predict he would become?
    a. A criminal
    b. A drummer
    c. A dustman
    d. A millionaire

19. When John first demonstrated how he plays to local drummer Gary Allcock, what was his first impression of John's playing?
    a. He was excellent.
    b. He was terrible.
    c. He played off rhythm.
    d. He played too hard.

20. Who was John Bonham's primary drumming role model as a child?
    a. Buddy Rich
    b. Max Roach
    c. Gene Krupa
    d. Art Blakey

ANSWERS

1. A- Robert. He is a few months younger than John Bonham. Jimmy is the elder statesman of the group.

2. C- Heston

3. D- It was around the house. Jimmy said, "I don't know whether [the guitar] was left behind by the people [in the house] before [us], or whether it was a friend of the family's—nobody seemed to know why it was there."

4. A- "Baby Let's Play House." Listen to that slick solo, and you will see why. It also has the line "I'd rather see you dead little girl than to be with another man," which the Beatles stole (I mean reappropriated) for the song "Run for Your Life."

5. C- They confiscated it. But luckily for us, they always gave it back.

6. False. He was on the show, but there was no competition!

7. A- Halesowen. Its main claim to fame is that it is one of the largest towns in the UK without a railway station. If you like the name, other great English town names include Great Snoring, Papplewick, and Over Peover.

8. B- His hair. Jimmy says he grew his hair like English rocker Jimmy Fury. Google it to get an idea. It's actually a pretty good look! As Plant said in an interview, "Hair. But not this Hair, the Hair of Billy Fury. Yeah, that's got to be the title of the fucking interview, hasn't it? The Hair of Billy Fury [laughs]. I loved Billy Fury, stunning, and that's why I just wanted to get that thing, that Billy Fury moment."

9. D- Accounting. It was his father's idea, but hey, if things don't work out with singing, he has something to fall back on. Though he never finished the program, every now and then, he would crunch the numbers and save Led Zeppelin some money. For example, when he figured out that if they got a private plane for world tours and slept on it, it would cost less than hotels.

10. B- Wolverhampton Wanderers FC. When they qualified for the Premier League in 2018, he appeared at a party the team held and played "Whole Lotta Love" and "The Liquidator," a song banned at Molineux (the Wolves stadium). It involves a good deal of cursing and intimidation. Plant is such a fan that he says it placed a strain on his marriage. "It played havoc with my marriage for a while," he said. "When we won the League

Cup in 1974, it took me three days to get home from Wembley to Worcestershire. I have not got a clue where I was. I know the Mayor of Wolverhampton received the team in official form, and I remember being there for a minute or two."

11. B- 16. He wanted to explore the Midlands music scene and moved from one band to another.

12. A- Kent. In Sidcup, to be precise.

13. False. Although he played his 1962 Fender Jazz Bass for many years, it was not the first bass he bought.

14. False. He never had any interest in guitar and was inspired by Charlie Mingus and other jazz bassists to pick up the bass guitar. He said, "I couldn't even play a six-string acoustic guitar when I started," he says. "I was just fascinated by bass work generally. I used to turn up the bass on my records and listen to the runs, and in time I just picked it up."

15. True—kind of. John was born John Richard Baldwin. However, legendary Rolling Stones manager Andrew Loog Oldham suggested that he change his name to John Paul Jones after he saw a movie poster alluding to the feature film of the same name. Therefore, technically he was named after a 1959 John Farrow movie (that is Mia

Farrow's father if you are wondering) with a 6.5 rating on IMDB.

16. C-15. They were called the Deltas.

17. True. His poor mother had to endure labor for 26 total hours. Then terror ensued when little John was born without a heartbeat. There was no doctor in the ward, so one had to be asked to come quickly. That doctor revived him. Somehow, he survived this ordeal to become a bouncy baby boy. The nurse declared it "a miracle."

18. C AND D- The headmaster wasn't sure what to make of this weird boy and declared, "He will either end up a dustman or a millionaire." He was right!

19. D- He played too hard. Garry later said, "I remember him playing on one of my snare drums and me saying, 'For Christ-sakes, John, take it steady!' I thought he was going to knock it through the floorboards. He certainly hit hard."

20. C- Gene Krupa. John first saw him play in the movie *The Benny Goodman Story*. His brother Michael says that "John went to see the film with his dad" and after that "Gene Krupa was god." John also loved a scene in the movie *Beat the Band* where he plays with sticks on boiler room steam pipes.

DID YOU KNOW?

- Robert Plant was an introspective loner of a child. Though he dreamed of becoming a rock star, he did not believe it was possible for such a shy boy. He would later recall that despite feeling like the constant outsider at school, his love for music made him feel like he belonged to something for the first time. As always, the catalyst was Elvis. As Plant remembered, "When I was a kid, I used to hide behind the curtains at home at Christmas, and I used to try and be Elvis. There was a certain ambiance between the curtains and the French windows. There was a certain sound there for a ten-year-old. That was all the ambiance I got at ten years old, and I always wanted to be a bit similar to that."

- A lot of the imagery in Led Zeppelin's best songs was inspired by his childhood in the Midlands. His grandmother Celia was Romani and loved to tell him local tales. For example, the May Queen in "Stairway to Heaven" is believed to have been inspired by a tradition from the Endon Well Dressing Festival, which takes place near

Birmingham. These stories also inspired the song "Battle of Evermore." Finally, "Black Country Woman" was written about the area.

- John Paul Jones is a very accomplished keyboard player because he played that instrument for years, well before he ever touched a bass. As a child, he played piano at home with his father, a well-known pianist and arranger for jazz big bands. He then started taking organ lessons and played at his local church regularly.

- John Bonham's love for the drums was instinctive. From the earliest point in his childhood, he would make drum sets out of coffee tins and anything else around the house that would make a pleasing noise.

CHAPTER II:

PRE-ZEPPELIN CAREERS

1. Jimmy got his first regular gig playing for singer Neil Christian in his band, The Crusaders. Why did he leave the band after two years?
   a. He was kicked out.
   b. He didn't like the music.
   c. He wasn't getting paid enough.
   d. He fell ill.

2. Jimmy became one of the premier studio guitarists in the United Kingdom in the early to mid-1960s. Which label first brought him in as their steady guy?
   a. EMI
   b. Decca
   c. Polydor
   d. MCA

3. John got a lot of gigs as a drummer in his teenage years. How did he get so many jobs?
   a. He was just that good.
   b. He was a charmer.
   c. He had connections.
   d. He was willing to pay bribes.

4. Before Band of Joy, Robert was in a few obscure bands. What was the name of the most bizarrely named one?
   a. Obbstweedle
   b. Hebbstweedle
   c. Hobbstweedle
   d. Frankentweedle

5. Robert didn't have many recordings before Led Zeppelin. However, he did lay down a couple of tracks with which cornerstone figure in British blues?
   a. John Mayall
   b. Alexis Korner
   c. Peter Green
   d. Spencer Davis

6. What was the name of the first band in which Robert and John Bonham played together?
   a. Band of Joy
   b. Crawling King Snakes
   c. Led Zeppelin
   d. A Way of Life

7. The Band of Joy is most famous for launching Robert Plant's career. However, bass guitarist David Pegg also had quite a career. Which of these acts DIDN'T feature his playing?
   a. Fairport Convention
   b. Blodwyn Pig
   c. Nick Drake
   d. Jethro Tull

8. One of the first bands John Paul Jones played in was called the Jett Blacks. Which legendary lead guitarist was also in that band?
   a. Peter Green
   b. John McLaughlin
   c. Jeff Beck
   d. Steve Howe

9. Which Rolling Stones album did John Paul Jones contribute memorable session work?
   a. Paint It Black
   b. She's a Rainbow
   c. Ruby Tuesday
   d. Gimme Shelter

10. Which of these classic songs by Scottish singer-songwriter Donovan did NOT feature work from John Paul Jones?
   a. "Season of the Witch"
   b. "Hurdy Gurdy Man"
   c. "Mellow Yellow"
   d. "Sunshine Superman"

11. Why did John Paul Jones give up his career as a session musician?
   a. He couldn't get work.
   b. He wanted to make his own music.
   c. He was exhausted.
   d. It didn't pay enough.

12. In one of his many special sessions, Jimmy Page played on the theme song to a James Bond movie. Which movie was it?

    a. *Goldfinger*

    b. *Thunderball*

    c. *You Only Live Twice*

    d. *Diamonds Are Forever*

13. Jimmy had a rival as the premier session guitar player in England in the mid-1960s. Who was the other one?

    a. Albert Lee

    b. John McLaughlin

    c. Big Jim Sullivan

    d. Joe Moretti

14. True or False: Jimmy played those gorgeous bluesy licks at the forefront of the version of "Baby Please Don't Go," released by Van Morrison and his band, Them.

15. On which of these singles did Jimmy play the 12-string guitar?

    a. The Kinks – "I'm a Lover Not a Fighter"

    b. Petula Clark – "Downtown"

c. Vashti Bunyan – "Some Things Just Stick in Your Mind"

d. The Who – "Bald Headed Woman"

16. In 1965 Jimmy played on the song "I Pity the Fool" for a young band called the Manish Boys. The band went nowhere. But their lead singer certainly didn't. Who was the precocious leading man?
   a. Marc Bolan
   b. David Bowie
   c. Elton John
   d. Tom Jones

17. True or False: Robert says his voice never sounded better than when he sang on the Band of Joy's debut album.

18. What was the name of the band John Bonham recorded his first song with?
   a. The Cardinals
   b. The Padres
   c. The Mariners
   d. The Senators

19. The Band of Joy did not have many recordings. However, one of them was a classic rock standard. Which song is it?
    a. "Hey Joe"
    b. "Yesterday"
    c. "California Dreamin'"
    d. "Nights in White Satin "

20. True or False: Robert was homeless when he met Jimmy Page.

ANSWERS

1. D- He fell ill. He got infectious mononucleosis.
2. B- Decca. However, he ended up playing for everybody, including adding guitar for the Beatles, the biggest stars on rival EMI. Some of his guitar work can be heard in the movie *A Hard Day's Night*.
3. A- He was just that good. His friend remembers, "We went out with him a couple of nights to see a band, and the first thing he'd say to me was, 'That drummer is crap.' When they came off for a break, he'd go straight up to the bandleader and say, 'Your drummer's not much good, is he? Let me have a go, and I'll show you.' He'd get on the drums, and everyone would be amazed. So the poor chap would get the sack, and John would take his job. He was pushy, and he got in wherever he wanted—but he had a heart of gold."

4. A- Obbstweedle. It is misspelled and misstated in many places, which is understandable.
5. B- Alexis Korner. The songs are "Steal Away" and "Operator" and they appear on the album *Musically Rich...and Famous.*
6. B- Crawling King Snakes. The two developed a mutual admiration and kept in touch. Therefore, when Robert formed Band of Joy, he asked John to join.
7. B- Blodwyn Pig. While Jethro Tull was a bigger band, he is a much more significant part of Fairport Convention's underrated body of work.
8. B- John McLaughlin.
9. B- "She's a Rainbow." If you listen to the song, that gorgeous string arrangement that swoops through it was written and arranged by John Paul Jones. Much of the album it was on, *Their Satanic Majesties,* was panned as a Beatles rip-off. However, that song stood out, at least partially because of his remarkable contribution.
10. A- "Season of the Witch." "Sunshine Superman" was practically a Led Zeppelin

song. Jimmy played lead guitar on it. Jimmy was introduced to Donovan by Mickie Most, who had produced some of the Animals and Herman Hermits' greatest hits. Donovan must have liked what he heard because he let Jimmy rip through a 30-second, 50s rock 'n' roll type solo. The song was one of the most important songs of the time because it was innovative in bringing psychedelic sound into the mainstream. The song hit #1 in the United States long before Led Zeppelin was a glimmer in Jimmy's eye. In 2011, Page reunited with Donovan to perform the song at the Royal Albert Hall in London.

11. C- He was exhausted. He was on so many songs; he would later say, "I can't remember three-quarters of the sessions I was on." Therefore, by 1968 he was crashing under the workload. "I was arranging 50 or 60 things a month, and it was starting to kill me." He thought joining a band might work out better for him.

12. A- *Goldfinger*. You can hear him strumming the acoustic guitar behind the loud orchestration on Shirley Bassey's title song.

13. C- Big Jim Sullivan. The other guitarists mentioned also picked up plenty of work. But the top choices at the time were either "small" Jimmy Page or "big" Jim Sullivan. The two were not really rivals since there was plenty of work to go round. The two played together on Dave Berry's classic single, "The Crying Game." Page also used Sullivan's Gibson J-200 acoustic guitar on *Led Zeppelin I*.

14. False. Jimmy played the rhythm guitar parts. Then-guitarist Billy Harrison played the lead parts. It is kind of amazing that after the band broke up, the talented guitarist remained confined to the local Belfast music scene.

15. A- The Kinks — "I'm a Lover, Not a Fighter." He uses the instrument to add drive and grittiness to the song. Dave Davies and Jimmy play off each other brilliantly.

16. B- David Bowie. Bowie does his best to sound like a standard blues-rock singer, and Jimmy already has his prime Zeppelin chops ready.

17. False. Robert did not sing on the Band of Joy's album. It came out in 1978 without the singer, who was already towards the end of his Led Zeppelin career. They invited Plant to contribute to the album, but it did not pan out.

18. D- The Senators. The name of the song was "She's A Mod." The bassist of the band, Bill Ford, recalled that one night their drummer didn't show up. The singer said he had a friend who could play. "He came back 20 minutes later with this lad named John Bonham. We started the second half, and it was as if someone had stuck rocket fuel in our drinks! We went down a storm, and John joined us as our drummer there and then."

19. A- "Hey Joe." Although it was performed and covered by many artists (we are still not sure who wrote it), Robert was clearly channeling the definitive version by Jimi Hendrix.

20. True. As Robert remembers it, "I had nowhere to live, and the keyboard player's dad had a pub in Wolverhampton with a spare room. The pub was right over the road

from Noddy Holder's father's window cleaning business, and Noddy used to be our roadie. We used to go to gigs with Noddy Holder's dad's buckets crashing around on top of the van! And that is when I met Pagey..." If you are paying attention, that is the second (and last) reference here to Noddy's father's crashing buckets.

DID YOU KNOW?

- One of the first times John Bonham was ever recorded in the studio did not go so well. When his band, A Way of Life, was recording a demo at Zella Studios, engineer Johnny Haynes said that John's drumming was "unrecordable" as he was just too loud. John did not forget this slight. He would later send Haynes a Led Zeppelin gold record with a note reading, "Thanks for the advice."

- Band of Joy had so many connections to rock history that even one of their roadies is a legend. Slade frontman Neville John Holder, better known as Noddy, was friends with Robert and would work as a roadie for more than one band he fronted. Noddy remembers that Robert would take girls into his van "with the window-cleaning ladders and buckets banging all around him." His band Slade would have several #1 singles and sell millions of albums worldwide.

- Jimmy played on an endless array of British hit singles in the 1960s. The most famous among them include The Who's first single "I Can't Explain," Marianne Faithfull's "As Tears Go By," The Rolling

Stones's "Heart of Stone," "Here Comes the Night" by Them, and Dave Berry's "The Crying Game." Probably his most famous session work is the lead guitar on Joe Cocker's version of "With a Little Help From My Friends." However, he didn't read music, so he did most of it by sheer instinct. He would later recall, "In the initial stages, they just said, play what you want, cause at that time I couldn't read music or anything."

- Jimmy Page formed a writing and recording partnership with remarkable singer-songwriter Jackie DeShannon in the mid-1960s. Aside from their professional relationship, the two also had an intense romantic relationship. It is believed, though not confirmed, that Jimmy wrote his beautiful love song "Tangerine" after their breakup in 1965. Jackie was one of the first female singer-songwriters in rock history and went on to have a successful career. She is best remembered for her stirring version of Burt Bacharach's song "What the World Needs Now Is Love."

- Perhaps the best session song Page ever played on also led to the name Led Zeppelin. The brilliant Jeff Beck had just left the Yardbirds and asked Jimmy to help put together a band for his first solo single.

Jimmy put together a band for the ages, bringing in Keith Moon of The Who, John Paul Jones, and playing rhythm guitar himself. The resulting song, known as "Beck's Bolero," was so good that the musicians contemplated starting a band together. Moon shot the project down, quipping that it would "go over like a lead balloon." That was the origin of the name that the band would eventually use.

CHAPTER III:

FROM THE NEW YARDBIRDS TO LED ZEPPELIN

1. True or False: Page was the first person the Yardbirds considered to replace Eric Clapton when he quit the band in March 1965.

2. Jimmy believed that the Yardbirds could have been better than the Stones or Cream, but instead, their potential remained unfulfilled. Who does he blame for that?
   a. Himself
   b. Keith Relf
   c. Chris Dreja
   d. Jeff Beck

3. John Bonham was not Page's first choice as drummer for the New Yardbirds. Instead, he had his eye on the drummer of which band?

a. Procol Harum

b. The Animals

c. The Small Faces

d. Spooky Tooth

4. What was the first time all four members of Led Zeppelin appeared on the same record?

   a. Led Zeppelin I

   b. P.J. Proby – "Jim's Blues"

   c. Jeff Beck – "Beck's Bolero"

   d. Yardbirds – *Live Yardbirds! Featuring Jimmy Page*

5. Which song did Plant sing for Jimmy in his audition for the New Yardbirds?

   a. The Animals – "The House of the Rising Sun"

   b. Roy Orbison – "Oh, Pretty Woman"

   c. Jefferson Airplane – "Somebody to Love"

   d. The Turtles – "Happy Together"

6. Why did Jimmy join the Yardbirds in 1966?

   a. He wanted better pay than he was getting in session work.

   b. He wanted creative freedom.

c. He was tricked into it.

d. He felt like he could do a better job than Jeff Beck.

7. True or False: Jimmy was not technically a full member of the Yardbirds.

8. How did the Yardbirds and Jeff Beck part ways?
   a. Jeff was fired.
   b. Jeff said it was either him or Page.
   c. Jeff left without saying he was quitting.
   d. Jeff announced he was going to the press.

9. Why did the Yardbirds break up?
   a. Jimmy wanted to move in a heavier direction.
   b. Keith Relf and Jim McCarty wanted to move on.
   c. They had severe legal troubles.
   d. The band was no longer successful.

10. When Jimmy was putting together the New Yardbirds, who was his first choice as a lead vocalist?
    a. Robert Plant

b. Steve Marriott

c. Terry Reid

d. Paul Rodgers

11. What was the first song the New Yardbirds played in their debut rehearsal?

a. "Over Under Sideways Down"

b. "Dazed and Confused"

c. "Train Kept A-Rollin'"

d. "Heart Full of Soul"

12. Where did the New Yardbirds play their first show?

a. Copenhagen

b. Oslo

c. Malmo

d. Stockholm

13. How long did it take to record the self-titled debut album?

a. 12 hours

b. 36 hours

c. Four days

d. A week

14. What role did the Atlantic record company play in the recording of the Led Zeppelin I?
    a. They were very hands-off.
    b. They micro-managed.
    c. They expected a hit single.
    d. They were not involved at all.

15. How much did it cost to record the debut album?
    a. £782
    b. £1,782
    c. £2,782
    d. £3,782

16. Jimmy is famous for using Gibson Les Paul guitars. However, on that first album, he used a 1959 Fender Telecaster through a Supro Thunderbolt to a devastating effect. Why did he stop using that sound?
    a. He thought it sounded tinny.
    b. It was no longer fashionable.
    c. It didn't sound good for rhythm parts.
    d. That guitar was ruined.

17. Jimmy didn't want to release any singles off the debut album. However, Atlantic insisted. Which song off the album was the first Led Zeppelin single?

    a. "Babe I'm Gonna Leave You"
    b. "Communication Breakdown"
    c. "Good Times Bad Times"
    d. "Dazed and Confused"

18. True or False: Robert Plant didn't write any of the songs on Led Zeppelin I.

19. The second song on the debut album, "Babe I'm Gonna Leave You," was a cover version. Whose version was the band covering?

    a. Anne Bredon
    b. Joni Mitchell
    c. Lulu
    d. Joan Baez

20. True or False: Page was an accomplished pedal steel guitar player and finally got to show it off on "Your Time is Gonna Come."

ANSWERS

1. True. Page was very well known for his session work, and Jeff Beck was virtually unknown. However, Page recommended him to The Yardbirds. It was not the first time they had offered him the job either. When Eric Clapton was still the lead guitarist, they tried to replace him, probably because they felt his ego was getting too big. "The very first time... [Yardbirds manager] Giorgio Gomelsky said that Eric was going to have a 'holiday,' and I could step in and replace him. The way he put it to me, it just seemed really distasteful, and I refused. Eric had been a friend of mine, and I couldn't possibly be party to that."

2. D- Jeff Beck. Jimmy has the utmost respect for Jeff's playing but has doubts about his personality. "It could have been even better than the Stones," Jimmy recalled. Maybe even more innovative than what Clapton was doing as a soloist in Cream. Could have, would have, should have... except for one thing: the self-destructive streak in Jeff that would also unhinge his later career with his own

Beck Group. As Jimmy said ruefully, "Jeff's his own worst enemy in that respect."

3. A- Procol Harum. Page was interested in the services of drummer B. J. Wilson. The drummer didn't even consider the offer. Procol Harum had just had a #1 hit, and the Yardbirds had been struggling for years. It was only when Wilson turned the guitarist down that Page turned to Bonham. Plant got into some hot water when he dismissed the late Wilson's talents in an interview.

4. B- P. J. Proby – "Jim's Blues." John Paul Jones had been hired to work on the song by American singer P. J. Proby before Led Zeppelin had been formed. However, by the time the session rolled around, the band had been created. Jones was always the consummate professional. Therefore, when the date came up for this session, he didn't bail. Instead, John asked his bandmates to help. Consequently, we get a truly Led Zeppelin-like cut on this one. If you are wondering, the Jim in the title is Proby himself, and not Jimmy. His given name is James Marcus Smith.

5. C- Jefferson Airplane – "Somebody to Love." Page recalled, "When I auditioned him and heard him sing, I immediately thought there must be

something wrong with him personality-wise or that he had to be impossible to work with, because I just could not understand why, after he told me he'd been singing for a few years already, he hadn't become a big name yet. So I had him down to my place for a little while, just to sort of check him out, and we got along great. No problems."

6. C- He was tricked into it. Jimmy had come to a Yardbirds show in Oxford. After a terrible drunken show, bassist Paul Samwell-Smith announced he was leaving the band. Jeff asked Jimmy to join as a bassist just for a little while until they found a replacement. But Beck had an ulterior motive. As he would later explain, "Jimmy wasn't a bass player. But the only way I could get him involved was by insisting that it would be okay for him to take over on bass for the band to continue. Gradually — within a week, I think — we were talking about doing dueling guitar leads." Soon they had switched rhythm guitarist Chris Dreja to bass, and Jimmy and Beck launched a brief but blistering cooperation.

7. True. Since he had only joined provisionally, he was paid a set wage rather than a share of profits like a

band member. However, his contract was a very good one. Page says, "I was only on a wage, anyway, with the Yardbirds. I'd like to say that because I was earning about three times as much when I was doing sessions, and I've seen it written that 'Page only joined the Yardbirds for the bread.' I was on wages except when it came to the point when the wages were more than what the rest of the band were making, and it was cheaper to give me what everybody else was getting."

8. C- Jeff left without saying he was quitting. As Page remembered, "One time in the dressing room, I walked in, and Beck had his guitar up over his head, about to bring it down on Keith Relf's head, but instead smashed it on the floor. Relf looked at him with total astonishment, and Beck said, 'Why did you make me do that?' Fucking hell. Everyone said, 'My goodness gracious, what a funny chap.' We went back to the hotel, and Beck showed me his tonsils, said he wasn't feeling well, and saw a doctor. He left for L.A., where we were headed in two days' time anyway. When we got there, though, we realized that whatever doctor he was claiming to see must have had his office in the Whiskey [the club on the Sunset Strip]. He was

actually seeing his girlfriend and had just used the doctor bit as an excuse to cut out on us."

9. B- Keith Relf and Jim McCarty wanted to move on. Jimmy was not ready to break up the band. He recalls, "It just got to a point where Relf and McCarty couldn't take it anymore. They wanted to go and do something totally different. When it came to the final split, it was a question of begging them to keep it together, but they didn't. They just wanted to try something new. I told them we'd be able to change within the group format. Coming from a sessions background, I was prepared to adjust to anything. I hated to break it up without even doing a proper first album."

10. C- Terry Reid. However, Terry had just signed a solo contract with Mickie Most and was slated to open for the Rolling Stones and Cream. Therefore, he suggested Page check out a young singer called Robert Plant. Page replied, "If he was so good, how come I'd never heard of him?"

11. C- "Train Kept A-Rollin'." Jimmy recalls, "It was unforgettable. Everybody just freaked. It was like these four individuals, but this collective energy made this fifth element. And that was it. It was

there immediately–a thunderbolt, a lightning flash–boosh! Everybody sort of went, 'Wow'..."

12. A- Copenhagen. To be more precise, the show took place at the Gladsaxe Teen Clubs in the Copenhagen suburb of Gladsaxe. About 1,200 fans turned up, and according to the local media, they were pretty happy with what they heard. A Danish newspaper reported, "Their performance and their music were absolutely flawless, and the music continued to ring nicely in the ears for some time after the curtains were drawn after their show. Therefore, we can conclude that the new Yardbirds are at least as good as the old ones were."

13. B- 36 hours. However, the studio time was not booked consecutively, and those hours were spread out thinly between 20 September and 10 October 1968. This schedule gave the band some time to rehearse and explains why the album sounded so smooth despite the minimal studio time.

14. D- They were not involved at all. Manager Peter Grant and Jimmy didn't want a record company to interfere. Jimmy said, "I wanted artistic control in a vise grip because I knew exactly what I wanted to do with these fellows. In fact, I financed and

completely recorded the first album before going to Atlantic."

15. B- £1,782. Not a bad investment! It gave Led Zeppelin a lot more leverage when negotiating with record companies.

16. D- That guitar was ruined. Rather than a purely stylistic choice, Jimmy was traumatized by what happened to his favorite ax. In 1998, he said, "I still have it, but it's a tragic story. I went on tour with the '59 Les Paul that I bought from Joe Walsh, and when I got back, a friend of mine had kindly painted over my paint job... His paint job totally screwed up the sound and the wiring, so only the neck pickup worked. I salvaged the neck and put it on my brown Tele string bender that I used in The Firm." After that incident, he decided to try something different. The result is his classic Les Paul through Marshall amps sound.

17. C- "Good Times, Bad Times." The single didn't do particularly well, peaking at #80 on the Billboard charts. This helped cement the bands' long-term reputation as the ultimate album act.

18. False. Robert participated in the writing process. However, he didn't receive any credit because he had a contract with CBS, which did not allow him

to receive any credits. He played a part in writing "Good Times, Bad Times," "Your Time Is Gonna Come," "Communication Breakdown," "Babe I'm Gonna Leave You," and "How Many More Times." Luckily for him, this also protected him from some of the lawsuits, which came out of that album from songwriters who believed they deserved credit for some of the songs.

19. D- Joan Baez. Page had been fascinated with the Baez version of the song for years before recording it. The guitarist remembered, "I used to do the song in the days of sitting in the darkness playing my six-string behind Marianne Faithfull." The arrangement is quite different from the one Baez used. It is far longer and uses the principles of "light and shade" that typify Page's arrangements and would have a massive influence on the future of hard rock.

20. False. He had never played before, and rather than hire someone else to play. It sounds pretty good to a rock audience, but a country connoisseur can tell it's an amateur playing. Page said, "I learned it for that session. We also had worked out a version of 'Chest Fever' in rehearsals, though we never played it onstage. That had an organ and pedal steel on it."

DID YOU KNOW?

- The band from "Beck's Bolero" came pretty close to fruition instead of the Led Zeppelin we know and love. As Page remembers, "We were going to form a group called Led Zeppelin at the time of 'Beck's Bolero' sessions with the lineup from that session. It was going to be me and Beck on guitars, Moon on drums, maybe Nicky Hopkins on piano. The only one from the session who wasn't going to be in it was Jonesy, who had played bass. Instead, Moon suggested we bring in Entwistle as bassist and lead singer as well, but after some discussion, we decided to use another singer. The first choice was Stevie Winwood, but it was decided that he was too heavily committed to Traffic at the time and probably wouldn't be too interested. Next, we thought of Steve Marriott. He was approached and seemed to be full of glee about it. A message came from the business side of Marriott, though, which said, 'How would you like to play guitar with broken fingers? You will be if you don't stay away from Stevie." After that, the idea sort of fell apart.

- You always hear that the band started the tour as the New Yardbirds to fulfill the Yardbirds' contract for a Scandinavian tour. The idea is that none of the Yardbirds wanted to continue and were sick of the band. However, this is not a completely accurate account. While most of the Yardbirds had no interest in continuing, bassist Chris Dreja did. As drummer Jim McCarty remembers, "Chris Dreja got shunted out in favor of John Paul Jones. But Chris had rights to the name. He stopped them from using The New Yardbirds, sent them a lawyer's letter or something. So legally, they couldn't carry on with it. They changed it to [Led] Zeppelin." Therefore, if it had not been for this legal action, Zeppelin may have remained the New Yardbirds. The name, of course, is a reference to the joke Keith Moon had made two years earlier about their chances of success.

- Jimmy did not write "Dazed and Confused," perhaps the best-known song on Led Zeppelin's debut album. However, for years he claimed that he did. The original version was written by Jake Holmes and appeared on his album *The Above Ground Sound of Jake Holmes*. While it is a very different arrangement, it is unmistakably the same song. Yardbirds drummer Jim McCarty explains how the song came to Jimmy's attention. He says the band was looking for new material. "We were quite stale and stuck creatively" when Page joined, Yardbirds drummer Jim McCarty remembers today. "We were still playing really similar things as we had with Jeff Beck. We had very few new things and running a bit low on ideas of songs to cover or songs that we wanted to do." When he heard "Dazed and Confused," he was enchanted by the ominous riff. "The following day, I went down and got his album at Bleecker Bob's record store," says McCarty. "I had a little record player on the road, and I played it to Jimmy and the guys and then we said, we should work out a version." At first, Holmes was not concerned, but over the years, as Led Zeppelin got bigger and bigger, he changed his mind. Holmes pretty accurately summed up the situation "by now, it's like if your baby is kidnapped at two years old and raised by another woman. All these years later, it's her kid." In 2010, Holmes and Page reached an agreement. The guitarist paid Holmes an undisclosed amount, and the credits on new releases read "By Jimmy Page; Inspired by Jake Holmes."

- *Rolling Stone's* review of *Led Zeppelin I* was brutal. The review savaged Jimmy as "a writer of weak, unimaginative songs" and Robert "as foppish as Rod Stewart, but he's nowhere near so exciting." The album was dismissed as an inferior copy of Cream and the Jeff Beck Group. The band never forgave the publication and always treated them with suspicion. Reportedly a few years later, *Rolling Stone* sent a freelancer to interview Page. When the guitarist asked him why they bothered, considering how much they disliked the band, the reporter responded, "When I used to work at a record store the running joke was that if you bought every album *Rolling Stone* thought was good you would have the worst record collection on the planet." The band loved the answer and cooperated with the interview.

- If you think that *Led Zeppelin I* sounds different from other albums of the time, you are right. The team of Jimmy Page and Glyn Johns pioneered and perfected several recording techniques in the studio. Page used a "distance makes depth" concept throughout the album to give the instrumentation depth and ambiance. While most engineers placed the microphones close to the amplifiers, Page kept a distance between them to capture the fullness of the sound. At times, they were kept as far as 20 feet away. He focused on creating reverb through the natural interaction of sound rather than as an artificial effect. This also allowed Page and Johns to record the *ambient sound*: the distance of a note's time-lag. All of these things added up to a very different approach to recording, and boy does the difference show. To maximize the benefit of its unique sound, *Led Zeppelin I* was one of the first albums to be released in stereo only.

CHAPTER III:
WHOLE LOTTA SOPHOMORE, NO SLUMP

1. What was the first song Robert wrote the lyrics for entirely on his own?
   a. "Living Lovin Maid (She's Just a Woman)"
   b. "Heartbreaker"
   c. "Thank You"
   d. "Whole Lotta Love"

2. How many different studios did the band use to record their sophomore effort?
   a. 2
   b. 7
   c. 13
   d. 19

3. "Whole Lotta Love" was a massive hit for the band. However, it has been accused of plagiarism. Which song is said to be remarkably similar to the distinctive tune?
   a. Willie Dixon – "You Need Love"

b. The Small Faces – "You Need Loving"

c. The Four Tops – "Baby I Need Your Loving"

d. Little Milton – "I Need Your Love So Bad"

4. Eddie Kramer produced the second album, starting a very productive association with the band. Which of these other classic albums was NOT produced or engineered by Kramer?

a. Jimi Hendrix – *Are You Experienced*

b. Kiss – *Alive!*

c. The Rolling Stones – *Exile on Main Street*

d. Humble Pie – *Performance Rockin' the Fillmore*

5. The Lemon Song was very popular with teenage boys for its overt sexual imagery. Which blues song did Led Zeppelin "borrow" the most provocative parts from?

a. Howlin' Wolf – "Killing Floor"

b. Robert Johnson – "Travelling Riverside Blues"

c. Bo Carter – "Banana in Your Fruit Basket"

d. Blind Boy Fuller – "Sweet Honey Hole"

6. *Led Zeppelin II* saw Jimmy launch his trademark Gibson Les Paul through Marshall stacks sound.

Which was the first song he ever recorded with that setup?

a. "Whole Lotta Love"

b. "Heartbreaker"

c. "Bring It on Home"

d. "Moby Dick"

7. Which guitarist sold Jimmy his famous 1958 starburst Les Paul guitar?

a. Eric Clapton

b. Joe Walsh

c. Carlos Santana

d. Peter Frampton

8. *Led Zeppelin II* provided many songs that appeared for years in their live repertoire. However, there was one song they disliked and refused to play. Which one was it?

a. "Ramble On"

b. "Living Lovin Maid (She's Just a Woman)"

c. "What is and What Should Never Be"

d. "Bring It on Home"

9. *Led Zeppelin II* has a very distinct album cover art. On what did artist David Juniper base the concept?
   a. The cover of his favorite book
   b. A picture of an air force squadron
   c. A Hells Angels portrait
   d. A book about pirates

10. *Led Zeppelin II* was a smash hit. Which album did it knock off the top spot in the US when it reached the top of the album chart?
   a. Simon & Garfunkel – *Bridge Over Troubled Water*
   b. Grateful Dead – *American Beauty*
   c. Cat Stevens – *Tea for the Tillerman*
   d. The Beatles – *Abbey Road*

11. The riff for "Whole Lotta Love" was so iconic that it was used as the theme for the British show *Top of the Pops*. In what year did they retire the song?
   a. 1978
   b. 1981
   c. 1988
   d. 1993

12. Jimmy was looking for a specific amplifier sound when he recorded "Whole Lotta Love." He used a Vox amplifier instead. Which act inspired his setup?

    a. Cream
    b. The Jimi Hendrix Experience
    c. The Beatles
    d. The Who

13. John Bonham got a very distinctive sound on the song "Ramble On." How was it achieved?

    a. He played the pipes.
    b. He played a coat rack.
    c. The drums were recorded in a creative way.
    d. He played a guitar case.

14. After the band's hectic schedule for the first two albums, they were determined to have a proper vacation. Therefore, they retreated to the famous Bron-Yr-Aur cottage. Where is located?

    a. Dorset, England
    b. Somerset, England
    c. Snowdonia, Wales
    d. Queen's View, Scotland

15. Robert was inspired to write the lyrics to "Immigrant Song" while on a trip to what country?

    a. Iceland

    b. Denmark

    c. Norway

    d. Sweden

16. Who originally recorded the song "Gallows Pole?"

    a. Robert Johnson

    b. Blind Lemon Jefferson

    c. Elmore James

    d. Leadbelly

17. While recording *Led Zeppelin III*, the band worked on several songs that would later appear on the future album *Physical Graffiti*. Which of these songs is NOT a product of those sessions?

    a. "Down by the Seaside"

    b. "The Rover"

c. "In the Light"

d. "Poor Tom"

18. A variety of pictures appear on the back cover of *Led Zeppelin III*. What are the images of?
    a. The band in Bron-Yr-Aur cottage
    b. The band in Headley Grange
    c. The band in Olympic Studios
    d. Each band member in their own home

19. True or False: After their first two albums had received some surprisingly bad reviews, their third album was the first to be well-received by critics.

20. True or False: Because of the acoustic elements in *Led Zeppelin III*, it was their first album not to reach #1 in the United States.

ANSWERS

1. B- "Thank You." He wrote this love song to his wife at the time, Maureen Plant (now Wilson). It gave Robert the confidence to become the primary songwriter for the band.

2. C- 13. They included locations in London, Los Angeles, Memphis, New York City, and Vancouver.

3. A AND B. Trick question. Led Zeppelin has been accused of plagiarizing both songs for this one. Steve Marriott, lead singer for the Small Faces, did not sue. However, he was pretty unhappy with it. He complained that "[Plant] sang it the same, phrased it the same, even the stops at the end were the same." Dixon was even less amused and sued the band in 1985. They settled for an undisclosed amount, and Dixon's name appeared on the credits from then on. To Plant's credit, he admits it. "Page's riff was Page's riff. It was there before anything else. I just thought, 'Well, what am I going to sing?' That was it, a nick. Now happily paid for. At the time, there was a lot of conversation about what

to do. It was decided that it was so far away in time and influence that... well, you only get caught when you're successful. That's the game."

4. C- The Rolling Stones – *Exile on Main Street*. Although he was an assistant engineer on some other Stone classics, such as *Beggars Banquet*. Eddie called *Led Zeppelin II* "the best hard rock album I was ever involved in, and it still sets the standard for rock bands."

5. B- Robert Johnson – "Travelling Riverside Blues." However, if you answered A, you are not entirely wrong. The song is a rearrangement of the Howlin' Wolf classic. However, the section about "squeeze me, baby, until the juice runs down my leg" was taken from the Robert Johnson song. You should also check out the other two songs because they are fabulous.

6. B- "Heartbreaker." However, Jimmy did not adopt Marshall's because he liked their sound. Instead, it was a question of convenience. He said that he preferred using a rarer amplifier, but the bands' road manager was unhappy with his choices. As Jimmy remembers, he was "getting really, really nervous about the

amplifier going down and not getting a replacement. So they're saying, well, everybody else has got Marshall's, so I went to Hiwatt [Custom 100s] before I went to the Marshall's. But then I did go to Marshall because what they'd said was absolutely true—if it broke down somewhere, you'd be able to find a shop that would have one. Once I'd done the second album, the Marshall is being used by the end of those tracks [recorded] in New York. I got those during that '69 tour. So maybe *Heartbreaker* was done on a Marshall. And that's how it stayed, with the Marshall cabinet all the way through."

7. B- Joe Walsh. We can thank the future Eagles guitarist for Led Zeppelin's trademark sound. Jimmy remembered, "I had been mainly using the Telecaster, both on stage and in the studio. We were at the Fillmore at the time, and Joe Walsh, who was then playing guitar with his outfit The James Gang, said he had a Gibson Les Paul for sale—a 1959 model. He wanted to sell it for five hundred dollars—a right price at the time. Once I started playing it, that was it."

8. B- "Living Lovin Maid (She's Just a Woman)." The song was about a groupie that followed the

group around in its earliest years. The band did not perform the number live, thinking it was dumb. However, Atlantic placed it as the B-side of "Whole Lotta Love." However, it has received a good deal of airplay by the neat manner in which it follows "Heartbreaker" on the album. Therefore, many radio stations have and continue to play the two songs in tandem.

9. B- A picture of an air force squadron. Not just any squadron, but the Jag Staffel Division of the Deutsche Luftstreitkräfte (German Air Force during World War I). The unit was the home of the legendary Red Baron (real name Manfred von Richthofen), the pilot ace who shot down 80 enemy planes. Juniper replaced four of the pilots' heads with photos of the band members.

10. D- The Beatles – *Abbey Road*. In fact, it knocked the Beatles masterpiece off first twice, after it made a comeback. *Led Zeppelin II* remained at the top for seven weeks in total.

11. B- 1981. The Led Zeppelin song was used as a theme song to reflect the dominant popularity of rock at the time. Until then, they had used instrumental music of little distinction to start

the show. In the early '80s, as rock went out of fashion, the song was replaced. However, *Top of the Pops* producers returned to their senses in 1998 and remixed the song as the opener. It was featured in the show, which is somehow still on the air to this day.

12. C- The Beatles. Jimmy remembers that he obtained the amps when Paul Samwell-Smith left his equipment behind when he left the Yardbirds. He picked up the Vox amplifier heads, which he then used for the legendary song. "The way that I heard about those amplifiers was The Beatles had them because they couldn't hear their instruments over all the screaming, so they wanted louder amplifiers, and Vox duly obliged." He whipped them out for the famous song and recalled, "I was using the Super Beatle amps with the [Rickenbacker] Transonic cabinets. That's exactly what's on 'Whole Lotta Love.'"

13. D- He played a guitar case.

14. C- Snowdonia, Wales. The name of the cottage means "hill of the gold" in Welsh. The gorgeous mountainous region, dotted with medieval castles and the history of long-gone Welsh

kingdoms, inspired the band. The cottage also did not have access to running water or electric power. This drastic change of setting from the high life they had been living inspired the transformation of musical direction in *Led Zeppelin III*.

15. A- Iceland. Robert explained, "We weren't being pompous... We did come from the land of the ice and snow. We were guests of the Icelandic government on a cultural mission. We were invited to play a concert in Reykjavik, and the day before we arrived, all the civil servants went on strike, and the gig was going to be canceled. The university prepared a concert hall for us, and it was phenomenal. The response from the kids was remarkable, and we had a great time. 'Immigrant Song' was about that trip, and it was the opening track on the album that was intended to be incredibly different."

16. D- Leadbelly. However, Page discovered the song through a different version. He heard it on the 1962 album *12 String Guitar*, released by acoustic guitarist Fred Gerlach. Page wrote his version while playing around with John Paul Jones' banjo, an instrument he had never picked

up before. The guitarist remembered, "I just picked it up and started moving my fingers around until the chords sounded right, which is the same way I work on compositions when the guitar's in different tunings."

17. C- "In the Light." "Poor Tom" appeared on *Coda*. Meanwhile, "Down by the Seaside" and "The Rover" appeared on *Physical Graffiti*.

18. D- Each band member in their own home. Page was unhappy with the cover concept for *Led Zeppelin III*. The guitarist had hired Zacron, known as the "king of the collage" for his previous work. The artist had not updated the band on his progress until very close to the release date. Jimmy says, "It got to the point where I had to say, 'Look, I have got to have this thing.' I was not happy with the final result—I thought it looked teeny-bopperish. We were on top of a deadline, so of course, there was no way to make any radical changes. There are some silly bits—little chunks of corn and nonsense like that." However, the original vinyl has some cool details. For example, there is an opening in the cover allowing you to spin the cardboard and choose which band member you can see.

When you place one, another picture of the band member pops up elsewhere.

19. False. The third album confused people due to the acoustic half. The reviews were somewhat mixed. *Rolling Stone* gave it a better review than it did for the first two albums (which was not hard). However, their critic Lester Bangs said that while the acoustic songs were good, all the heavy songs sounded the same. Others accused them of ripping off Crosby, Stills & Nash. Page stopped giving interviews for well over a year because the reviews upset him.

20. False. False on two counts, actually. The debut album did not make #1 in the US. Also, *Led Zeppelin III* did reach the top in both the US and the UK.

DID YOU KNOW?

- *Led Zeppelin I* was such a smash success that Atlantic Records was pressing the band to complete a follow-up before they had proper studio time. The pressure on Jimmy was so significant that he almost caved under it. The band's road manager Richard Cole said, "I could see the battle fatigue taking its toll on Jimmy. His face seemed drawn. The circles under his eyes were getting darker. He started smoking more cigarettes than usual."

- Led Zeppelin never really carved out a serious amount of time to record *Led Zeppelin II*. Instead, most of it was recorded while touring behind the first album. Therefore, each song was separately recorded, mixed, and edited. Bonham recalled, "I remember we went out to the airport to meet our wives, got them back to the hotel, and then went straight back to the studio and did 'Bring It on Home.' We did a lot that year like that." As the band did not take much time to write, many of the songs were improvised onstage during some of the extended jams the bands' concerts featured at that time. In particular, they came up with a lot of material during their live versions of 'Dazed and Confused.' John Paul Jones said, "We'd remember the good stuff and dart into a studio along the way." Some of the studios they used were first-rate, such as Mystic Studios in LA. Meanwhile, they described the facilities in Vancouver as "the hut." Engineer Eddie Kramer recalled, "We cut some of the tracks in some of the most bizarre studios you can imagine...but in the end, it sounded bloody marvelous...there was one guy in charge, and that was Mr. Page."

- Jimmy was not confident about the album because of the haphazard way it was recorded. "It was quite insane, really," Page said. "We had no time, and we had to write numbers in hotel rooms. By the time the album came out, I was really fed up with it. I'd just heard it so many times in so many places. I really think I had lost confidence in it." However, it blew up and made Led Zeppelin one of the biggest bands in the world. "Our whole lives changed," Plant said. "It was such a sudden change we weren't sure how to handle it."

- The band started the recording for *Led Zeppelin III* in Olympic Studios in London. However, they were feeling uninspired. That is why they chose to go to the country and literally unplug. After developing their new songs at Bron-Yr-Aur cottage, the band needed electricity to rehearse them. However, they had no interest in returning to the city just yet. Therefore, they went out to Headley Grange. This building in Hampshire had served as a workhouse for the poor in the 19th century. It now often served as a country getaway and rehearsal space for the rock bands of the era. Page credits Headley Grange as the source of many of Zeppelin's innovations: "The reason we went there in the first place was to have a live-in situation where you're writing and really living the music. We'd never really had that experience before as a group, apart from when Robert [Plant] and I had gone to Bron-Yr-Aur. But that was just me and Robert going down there and hanging out in the bosom of Wales and enjoying it. This was different. It was all of us really concentrating in a concentrated environment, and the essence of what happened there manifested itself across three albums." Those subsequent three albums were *Led Zeppelin IV*, *Houses of the Holy*, and *Physical Graffiti*.

CHAPTER IV:

PEAK ZEPPELIN

1. Who played the piano on the song "Rock and Roll?"

    a. John Paul Jones

    b. Ian Stewart

    c. Nicky Hopkins

    d. Chuck Leavell

2. The song "Black Dog" is named after a real canine. Who owned the dog?

    a. Robert Plant

    b. Peter Grant

    c. Andy Johns

    d. No one knows

3. Who sings the beautiful female vocal parts on the song "Battle of Evermore?"

    a. Sandy Denny

    b. Joan Armatrading

    c. Linda Ronstadt

d. Carly Simon

4. Which guitar did Jimmy use to record the legendary solo on "Stairway to Heaven?"
   a. His Gibson EDS-1275 Doubleneck
   a. His '59 Les Paul
   b. His '59 Fender Telecaster
   c. His 1964 Fender Stratocaster

5. The first three Led Zeppelin albums were titled. Sort of. So were the rest. Why wasn't the fourth album given a title?
   b. They wanted the music to speak for itself.
   c. A jab at the critics
   d. They couldn't agree on a name.
   e. An editing mistake

6. How did the band capture that magnificently huge drum sound on the song "When the Levee Breaks?"
   a. They recorded it from far away.
   b. They placed the drums in the basement.
   c. They put a lot of reverb on the track.
   d. They set the drums in the stairwell.

7. True or False: The song "When the Levee Breaks" was initially written by blues duo Kansas Joe McCoy and Memphis Minnie. Therefore, Jimmy was later sued for copyright infringement on the song.

8. The song "Going to California" was inspired by a crush Robert Plant had. Which famous woman was he writing about?
   a. Cher
   b. Joni Mitchell
   c. Mia Farrow
   d. Jane Fonda

9. Which classic 1980s teen flick includes the quote, "When it comes down to making out, whenever possible, put on Side One of *Led Zeppelin IV*."
   a. *Fast Times at Ridgemont High*
   b. *Sweet Sixteen*
   c. *The Breakfast Club*
   d. *Say Anything*

10. Who had a song named "Stairway to Heaven" before Led Zeppelin did?
    a. Johnny Mathis

b. Neil Sedaka

c. Neil Diamond

d. Pat Boone

11. True or False: "Stairway to Heaven" was the most played song on American radio in the 1970s.

12. True or False: *Led Zeppelin IV* is one of the top-ten bestselling albums of all time.

13. The memorable cover of *Houses of the Holy* is based on a photograph taken at what location?
    a. Cappadocia, Turkey
    b. Giant's Causeway, Northern Ireland
    c. Crater Lake, Oregon
    d. Kermadec Islands, New Zealand

14. True or False: The band hated the first idea the graphics company came up with for the cover of the album.

15. The opening track of *Houses of the Holy*, "The Song Remains the Same," has a tricky rhythm

and is difficult to sing over. Why did Jimmy write it that way?

a. He wanted to challenge Robert.

b. Robert asked for a challenge.

c. It started out as a practical joke.

d. It started out as an instrumental.

16. Jimmy decided to write "The Rain Song" after a well-known colleague complained that Led Zeppelin never did any ballads. Who made the inaccurate complaint?

a. George Harrison

b. Eric Clapton

c. Pete Townshend

d. Jeff Beck

17. "The Crunge" is an atypically humorous song. In one of the funniest parts, Robert affectionately imitates a soul legend. Who is he imitating?

a. Sam Cooke

b. James Brown

c. Wilson Pickett

d. Otis Redding

18. Which song of the album became a Top 20 hit in the United States?

    a. "Over the Hills and Far Away"

    b. "The Crunge"

    c. "D'yer Mak'er"

    d. "The Ocean"

19. True or False: The *Rolling Stone* magazine panned this classic album as well.

20. Eddie Kramer and Led Zeppelin renewed their partnership after they had a massive falling out while recording *Led Zeppelin III*. What did they fight over?

    a. Plumbing equipment

    b. Indian food

    c. Racehorses

    d. The conflict in Northern Ireland

ANSWERS

1. B- Ian Stewart. The song was written quickly in the style of 1950s rock. Stewart, who played piano on many Stones songs, was known for his fantastic ability in the genre. You can hear him with Zeppelin again on "Boogie with Stu."

2. D- No one knows. The dog was a Labrador retriever that wandered around Headley Grange. The band befriended the dog and named the song after him because they didn't have a better name. As for the meaning of the song, Robert says, "Not all my stuff is meant to be scrutinized. Things like 'Black Dog' are blatant, let's-do-it-in-the-bath type things, but they make their point just the same."

3. A- Sandy Denny. Robert was a huge fan of the lead singer from Fairport Convention. Her performance on the song is a reminder of her tremendous unfulfilled performance. Sandy remains the only female voice to ever appear on a Led Zeppelin album.

4. C- His '59 Fender Telecaster. Jimmy broke out the classic Telecaster Jeff had given him for the

solo. He used it rarely after the debut album, but here he used it to a devastating effect. The magazine *Guitar World* ranked it #4 on its all-time solo list.

5. B- As a jab at the critics. Jimmy says, "After all we had accomplished, the press was still calling us a hype. So that is why the fourth album was untitled." He wanted to show that the band had music that could speak for itself.

6. D- They placed the drums in the stairwell. The drums were one of the reasons the song was recorded several times before they finally got the masterful final take at Headley Grange. Led Zeppelin biographer George Case explains, "People wonder how that sounds so planetary, but there was a natural echo there, and then they put more on it. They also slowed it down in the mix, so it sounded really booming and had this huge reverb. It's almost physical when you listen to it." They could not get the vast sound Page envisioned at a studio session. The studio version was so powerful that the band found the song difficult to recreate live. They only played it a handful of times in 1975.

7. False. The song is credited to Page, Plant, Jones, Bonham, and Memphis Minnie. As the band was evolving musically, they also grew up and started giving the original writers the credit they deserved.

8. B- Joni Mitchell. Robert remains a huge fan. "That's the music that I play at home all the time, Joni Mitchell," Page said. "The main thing with Joni is that she's able to look at something that's happened to her, drawback and crystallize the whole situation, then write about it. She brings tears to my eyes—what more can I say?"

9. A- *Fast Times at Ridgemont High*. Led Zeppelin fanatic Cameron Crowe directed the movie.

10. B- Neil Sedaka. It reached #9 in the charts in 1960. Neil said in 2021, "You can't copyright a title, so Led Zeppelin, I forgive you!"

11. True. Radio stations asked Atlantic for a shorter version of the song. However, the band wouldn't budge. Therefore, radio stations played the entire 8-minute song. Good for them. What can you cut on that perfect song?

12. True, if you don't include compilations. With 37 million albums sold globally, there are few

albums ahead of it: Michael Jackson – *Thriller*, AC/DC – *Back in Black*, Meat Loaf – *Bat Out of Hell*, Pink Floyd – *Dark Side of the Moon*, Fleetwood Mac – *Rumors* and…Shania Twain – *Come on Over*.

13. B- Giant's Causeway, Northern Ireland. All the answers refer to areas with gorgeous volcanic eruption remains. A location in Peru was also considered. Stefan Gates, who designed the cover, never listened to the album until he did a BBC special on the cover in 2010.

14. True. The first idea was a tennis racket on a background of an electric green court. Jimmy remembers, "I said, 'What the hell does that have to do with anything?' And he said, 'Racket—don't you get it?' I said, 'Are you trying to imply that our music is a racket? Get out!' We never saw him again… That was a total insult—racket. He had some balls!"

15. D- It started out as an instrumental. Jimmy remembers, "It was originally going to be an instrumental—an overture that led into 'The Rain Song.' But I guess Robert had different ideas. You know, 'This is pretty good. Better get some lyrics—quick!' [laughs]… I had all the

beginning material together, and Robert suggested that we break it down into half-time in the middle. After we figured out that we were going to break it down, the song came together in a day."

16. A- George Harrison. George saw the band play and was apparently amazed by the quality of the performance. However, he observed that they had no ballads. Jimmy remembers thinking, "I'll give [Harrison] a ballad." As a nod to George, Jimmy inserted a small quote of one of his best-known songs. Jimmy says, "You'll notice I even quote 'Something' in the ['Rain Song's'] first two chords."

17. B- James Brown. In many of Brown's best early songs, he gives loud instructions to the band, such as "take it to the bridge." Plant pays tribute to this by mimicking him and then ends the song with "where's that confounded bridge?" The joke being that the oddly constructed piece notably does not have a bridge. The band performed a special version of the song in 1975, turning it into a cover of Brown's "Sex Machine."

18. C- "D'yer Mak'er." The band recorded the song as a joke, but Atlantic thought it had hit potential, and they were right. The silly reggae song was named as a parody of what the word Jamaica sounds like with a heavy English accent. It refers to the following joke: "My wife's gone to the <u>West Indies</u>." "Jamaica?" (Which, in an English accent, sounds like "Did you make her?") "No, she wanted to go."

19. True. The review read, "*Houses of the Holy* is one of the dullest and most confusing albums I've heard this year." It continues, "Their earliest successes came when they literally stole blues licks note for note, so I guess it should have been expected that there was something drastically wrong with their own material." The review urged the band to stick to their *blues-rock* roots. "Until they do, Led Zeppelin will remain Limp Blimp."

20. B- Indian food. Led Zeppelin was recording at Electric Ladyland Studios, the iconic recording site Kramer had built with Jimi Hendrix. As Eddie remembers it, "The band ordered some Indian food, and a whole bunch of it spilled on the floor," Kramer said. "I asked the roadies to

please clean it up. The studio was brand new, and I had a lot of pride in it. Suddenly [Led Zeppelin] are yelling, 'You don't tell our roadies what to do!' And they pulled out; they left, and I didn't speak to them for about a year!"

DID YOU KNOW?

- Even though *Led Zeppelin III* was not as successful as the sophomore album, the band used it as a blueprint to prepare their classic fourth album. Therefore, they returned to the house in Brun-Yr-Aur and practiced at Headley Grange again. They had considered using Mick Jagger's home in Stargroves, but the singer charged too much. Instead, they rented the legendary Rolling Stones Mobile Studio and placed it on Headley Grange. As Page remembers, "We needed the sort of facilities where we could have a cup of tea and wander around the garden and go in and do what we had to do." One of the best things about the property was that there was no entertainment or alcohol around, leaving them focused on recording.

- Led Zeppelin did more than just not title their fourth album. That was not all that dramatic. After all, they had barely bothered to title the first three albums. However, they also didn't have the band's name anywhere on the cover or any band pictures. Instead, all you saw was a picture of an older man carrying a bunch of sticks. The picture looks decidedly rural. However, when you open the complete packaging, you can see that the old man is standing up against a modern apartment building. It is a great statement but an odd marketing choice. Yet, the album sold 23 million copies.

- When Led Zeppelin first played their most famous song, "Stairway to Heaven," it was not well received. Jones remembers, "The first time we played 'Stairway' live, it was like, 'Why aren't they playing "Whole Lotta Love?"' Because people like what they know. And then 'Stairway' became what they knew." Robert also remembers being discouraged by seeing "people settling down to have 40 winks." That is just a reminder that when a band is debuting new material, you may be hearing a classic in the making!

- The album is known for having four rune symbols, each representing one of the band members. While fans at the time put a lot of effort into deciphering them, it appears that the band mostly did not. Jimmy remembers, "At first I wanted just one symbol on it, but then it was decided that since it was our fourth album and there were four of us, we could each choose our own symbol." Jimmy's symbol is an ancient representation of Saturn, which rules over Capricorn, Page's astrological sign. Jones picked a symbol representing competence and confidence. Bonham's sign represents the trinity of mother, father, and child. However, he may have chosen it because of its resemblance to the logo for Ballantine beer. Meanwhile, Robert chose the symbol of the Egyptian goddess of justice and fairness.

- *Houses of the Holy* had the most sophisticated musical arrangements of any Led Zeppelin album up to that point. That was partially a matter of musical growth. However, Jimmy and Jones had also developed sophisticated home studio setups. Therefore, Jimmy was able to present the band with complete visions of "The Rain Song" and "Over the Hills and Far Away." Meanwhile, Jones brought an advanced version of the song "No Quarter."

CHAPTER V:
LET'S GET
PHYSICAL. GRAFFITI

1. In 1973 the band formed its own record company, Swan Song. What was the biggest act on their label aside from Led Zeppelin?
   a. Bad Company
   b. Humble Pie
   c. Wishbone Ash
   d. Jethro Tull

2. True or False: The Rover was initially an acoustic song recorded during the *Led Zeppelin III* session.

3. True or False: *Physical Graffiti* was so successful that when it was released, all of the previous Led Zeppelin albums re-entered the Billboard Top 200.

4. Who played the song "In My Time of Dying" before Led Zeppelin did their version?

a. Bob Dylan

b. Blind Willie Johnson

c. Charlie Patton

d. Rev. B. J. Hill

5. *Physical Graffiti* was initially supposed to be a single album. How many songs were slated to be on the single LP release?

a. 8

b. 9

c. 10

d. 11

6. The band had heard that the mother of a deceased rock star was poverty-stricken and was not receiving royalties for her son's hits. Therefore, they gave credits to the mother for one of the songs on the album. Who was the singer?

a. Buddy Holly

b. Richie Valens

c. Big Bill Broonzy

d. The Big Bopper

7. The apartment block used on the cover of *Physical Graffiti* is a rock 'n' roll landmark. It is also associated with another great band. Which one?

   a. The Who

   b. Queen

   c. The Rolling Stones

   d. The Allman Brothers Band

8. Robert tried to record the vocals to the song "Black Country Woman" outdoors. However, his plans were foiled when he was attacked by which animals?

   a. Geese

   b. Foxes

   c. Deer

   d. Dogs

9. The song "Trampled Under Foot" had a working title, which was a nod to one of the band's favorite drinks. What was it called?

   a. Gin & Tonic

   b. Brandy & Coke

   c. Black & Tan

   d. Tom & Jerry

10. On what instrument does John Paul Jones play that distinctive keyboard part on "Trampled Under Foot?"
    a. Electric piano
    b. Moog synthesizer
    c. Clavinet
    d. Hammond Organ

11. Which song from *Physical Graffiti* did Robert later cover with Tori Amos?
    a. "Kashmir"
    b. "In the Light"
    c. "Ten Years Gone"
    d. "Down by the Seaside"

12. Jimmy was with Robert and the Plant family not long before the car crash that injured the singer. Where did he go just before the accident, possibly avoiding involvement?
    a. Athens
    b. Sicily
    c. Crete
    d. Cyprus

13. Plant recorded *Presence* with some severe injuries. During the recording, he almost crippled himself yet again. When did the accident occur?
    a. He fell while getting carried away with the vocals.
    b. He injured himself trying to mix a song.
    c. He fell while going to listen to a playback.
    d. John Bonham inadvertently pushed him.

14. Where did Jimmy and Robert meet up to write the songs for the *Presence* album?
    a. Headley Grange, England
    b. Malibu, California
    c. The Commonwealth of the Bahamas
    d. Marrakesh, Morocco

15. Which song on the album had the depressing working name, "the Wheelchair Song," because it reflected Robert's bad experiences?
    a. "Nobody's Fault but Mine"
    b. "Royal Orleans"
    c. "Tea for One"
    d. "Achilles Last Stand"

16. The song "Candy Store Rock" is a loving pastiche of 1950s rock 'n' roll. It was developed during jam sessions in that style the band would play live during live shows. What song was the platform for these sections in their concerts?

    a. "Whole Lotta Love"

    b. "Over the Hills and Far Away"

    c. "Black Dog"

    d. "Dazed and Confused"

17. The song "Royal Orleans" is about "A man I know." Who is Plant singing about?

    a. Himself

    b. Jimmy Page

    c. John Bonham

    d. John Paul Jones

18. During the recording of *Presence*, Bonham's alcoholism was spinning out of control. He punched an acquaintance in the face when she looked at him, and he did not recognize her. Where did this incident occur?

    a. The Burgundy Room

    b. The Rainbow Bar & Grill

    c. The Whisky A Go-Go

d. The Troubadour

19. Jimmy insisted that they leave LA and fly to Munich to finish the album in the middle of recording. Why did he do so?
    a. The sessions were going badly.
    b. Bonham was drinking too much.
    c. It had better facilities for Robert's temporary handicap.
    d. A thunderstorm spooked him.

20. When promoting *Presence*, John Bonham walked on stage in the middle of a show and insulted one of the members. Which band was it?
    a. Deep Purple
    b. The Eagles
    c. Aerosmith
    d. Fleetwood Mac

ANSWERS

1. A- Bad Company. That band recorded most of their biggest hits for the Swan Song label. Even though Led Zeppelin created the label to break free from Atlantic, they used their old record company to distribute in the United States.
2. True. The song was recorded in May 1970 at Headley Grange in an acoustic version. However, it didn't quite work. They recorded a hard-rocking version for *Houses of the Holy* but were not entirely happy with it. Then Jimmy added some overdubs and fixed it up for release on *Physical Graffiti*.
3. True.
4. Trick question. They all recorded it. No one knows who wrote the song since it is a traditional hymnal. Therefore, although Led Zeppelin credits themselves for writing it, they had no legal problems as a result.
5. A- 8. "Custard Pie," "In My Time of Dying," "Trampled Under Foot," "Kashmir," "In the Light," "Ten Years Gone," "Wanton Song," and "Sick Again" would have made up the album. However, they were too long for a single album and yet too

short for a double. Therefore, the band added several cuts they had from previous sessions to round it out.

6. B- The Richie Valens. The song "Boogie With Stu" is a pretty straightforward cover of "Ooh My Head," which Valens recorded a few months before his untimely death in a plane crash. However, the singer's mother, Concepcion "Concha" Valenzuela, tried to sue the band because she believed that the credit should be given over to her son completely, while the band, as is their custom, put their names in there.

7. C- The Rolling Stones. The apartments are located in Manhattan yet feature memorably in the visual work of two British bands. The famous video for the Stones song "Waiting for a Friend" was filmed using the same building, located on 96 and 98 St. Mark's Place.

8. A- Geese. Robert tried to record tracks indoors after that.

9. B- Brandy & Coke. A rough mix with that title appears on the remastered release of *Physical Graffiti*.

10. C- Clavinet. It is an amplified clavichord made in Germany, which was discontinued in the early 80s.

Jones says the part was inspired by Stevie Wonder's "Superstition," which also uses the clavinet alongside a Moog synthesizer.

11. D- "Down by the Seaside." Tori saw Robert as a mentor and recalls, "I was listening to Led Zeppelin as a kid, and then I worked with Robert in the early 90s. To work with somebody you've grown up listening to is a very different experience to working with a peer—in a way, you're in the same graduating class, you have a different relationship, you learn together. Whereas he was a mentor to me—he gave me advice on things I didn't even know would happen yet. Particularly to do with record labels and how the music business worked, and what to prepare for, and how to protect myself. That was invaluable."

12. B- Sicily. He was going to visit Aleister Crowley's old Abbey of Thelema. Due to Jimmy's interest in the occult figure, he considered buying the Abbey.

13. C- He fell while going to listen to a playback. Plant's leg crumpled under him, and he had to be rushed to a hospital. Plant recalls, "Fuck! I screamed. 'Not again! Not again!' I'd never known Jimmy to move so quickly." Robert later recalled, "He was out of the mixing booth and holding me up, fragile as he

might be, within a second. He became quite Germanic in his organization of things, and instantly I was rushed off to hospital again in case I'd reopened the fracture."

14. B- Malibu, California. At the time, Robert was a tax exile from England, only allowed to spend 30 days in the UK. Therefore, he spent his recuperation time avoiding the British Isles. Though Plant was in a dark place, Malibu did him good. He took therapeutic strolls along the beach with a cane. Jimmy and Robert even went to the Santa Monica Civic to see Donovan.

15. D- "Achilles Last Stand." Jimmy saw the song as aiming for something grandiose, saying he wanted to evoke "the façade of a gothic building with layers of tracery and statues." However, to Robert, it was far more personal. Achilles was a mythological hero with only one vulnerability, his heel. And, of course, Robert had broken his.

16. B- "Over the Hills and Far Away." Starting as a short live number, it began to incorporate rockabilly and other 1950s oriented genres. Plant didn't particularly like *Presence*. However, he feels "Candy Store Rock" is one of the "saving graces" of the album.

17. D- John Paul Jones. While not everything in the song actually happened, the story refers to something that happened in New Orleans to the bassist. Jones was hanging out with a well-known drag queen named Stephanie. Late that night, after smoking a joint in his room at the Royal Orleans, Jones and Stephanie fell asleep. The bassist remembers, "We rolled a joint or two, and I fell asleep and set fire to the hotel room, as you do, haha. And when I woke up, it was full of firemen!"

18. B- The Rainbow Bar & Grill. The Rainbow is one of the great rock haunts and was Zeppelin's favored LA watering hole. That night John had ordered 20 black Russians (vodka and coffee liqueur). He swiveled on his seat and spotted Michelle Myer, whom he had met several times before. She was eating dinner and smiled at the drummer. Bonham took this the wrong way, walked over, and punched her in the face before yelling, "Don't ever look at me that way again!"

19. B- He was spooked by a thunderstorm. Jimmy took his occult studies too seriously, or the cocaine made him paranoid, and he insisted the band leave after a bad thunderstorm over Malibu.

20. A- Deep Purple. He walked on stage at Nassau Coliseum and declared, "My name is John Bonham of Led Zeppelin, and I just wanna tell you that we got a new album comin' out called *Presence* and that it's fucking great! And as far as Tommy Bolin is concerned, he can't play for shit..." Not his finest moment, and as anyone who has heard "Spectrum" or "Come Taste the Band" can affirm: not remotely true.

DID YOU KNOW?

- During the recording of *Physical Graffiti*, John Paul Jones almost left the band. He left the initial recording sessions at Headley Grange. The band brought in Bad Company and finished their classic debut album because Led Zeppelin could not use the time booked. The band had become the biggest in the world, but the amount of touring and recording it had taken to get there was a massive strain on the quiet and family-oriented Jones. "We were all exhausted and under pressure, and it just came to a head," Jones said. "I didn't want to harm the group, but I didn't want my family to fall apart, either. I thought the band would be fun for a few years," Jones told Mojo. "I needed to do something musically free and fun and liberating, [...] but then I'd get back to the more serious career in the studio." Manager Peter Grant was worried the band would fall apart. However, to his relief, when Jones rejoined the band: "I think he realized he was doing something he really loved," Grant said, "It was never discussed again."

- While John Paul Jones was feeling uninspired, Jimmy was raring to go. The band took the most extended break it had ever had between albums: two long years. Jimmy later said, "I was basically musically salivating on the way there." The hunger showed. "All of us knew that it was a monumental piece of work, just because of the various paths that we'd trodden along to get to this. It was like a voyage of discovery, a topographical adventure." It was that hunger that led them to record more material than would fit on a single album. Jimmy is particularly proud of the flawless take of "In My Time of Dying" that appears on the record. "There were no edits or drop-ins or overdubs to the version you hear. This is Led Zeppelin just going for it for an 11-minute song with all the changes in it and everything and the musical map that you have to remember when it goes 1-2-3-4, tapes rolling."

- Led Zeppelin was on top of the world when *Physical Graffiti* was released. However, Robert's luck soon changed for the worse. He was vacationing with his family in Rhodes, Greece, when he lost control of their rented car. The children were fine, luckily, but both Robert and his wife Maureen sustained some nasty injuries. For a while, it didn't seem like Maureen would survive. She had sustained severe concussions, and her leg was broken in several places. The island did not have a suitable hospital or supplies. Maureen had lost a lot of blood and had a rare blood type. She needed a transfusion, but the process was very slow. There was just a single doctor on duty at the Greek hospital. Therefore, the Swan Song record company flew in a chartered jet equipped with stretchers, blood plasma, and two doctors from an English medical center. Robert Plant broke an ankle and elbow. Indeed, they wouldn't fully heal for about two years. The singer even had to spend a few months in a wheelchair. The accident affected Plant badly and significantly delayed the follow-up album and subsequent tours.

- The entire band had participated in the writing for years, especially from *Houses of the Holy* and onward. However, the music on *Presence* was written almost entirely by Jimmy. Robert handled the lyrics as usual. However, Jones and Page disagree on why the rest of the band was shut out of the writing process. Jimmy says he had no choice but to pick up the slack. He said, "Nobody else really came up with song ideas. It was really up to me to come up with all the riffs, which is probably why [the songs were] guitar-heavy. But I don't blame anybody. We were all kind of down." But Jones remembers it differently. "It became apparent that Robert and I seemed to keep a different time sequence to Jimmy. We just couldn't find him." Jones added that he "drove into SIR Studios every night and waited and waited... I learned all about baseball during that period, as the World Series was on, and there was not much else to do but watch it." He concluded, "The main memory of that album is pushing Robert around in the wheelchair from beer stand to beer stand. We had a laugh, I suppose, but I didn't enjoy the sessions, really. I just tagged along with that one."

CHAPTER VI:
A DARK CODA

1. Where did Led Zeppelin play their last show ever in the United States?
   a. Cincinnati, Ohio
   b. Miami, Florida
   c. Dallas, Texas
   d. Oakland, California

2. At that show, manager Peter Grant and Led Zeppelin security employee John Bindon were arrested after beating up a security staff member at the venue. Why did they attack him?
   a. He had a fight with Grant's son.
   b. He wouldn't honor a groupie's backstage pass.
   c. He confiscated drugs.
   d. It was a random attack.

3. Where did the band record the album *In Through the Out Door*?

   a. Copenhagen, Denmark

   b. Stockholm, Sweden

   c. Oslo, Norway

   d. Helsinki, Finland

4. What did the band do on weekends while recording their final album?

   a. Had drinking parties

   b. Played at a local bar

   c. Flew back to England

   d. Stayed in the mansion of an ABBA member

5. The band released one single off *In Through the Out Door*. Which song was it?

   a. "Fool in the Rain"

   b. "All My Love"

   c. "I'm Gonna Crawl"

   d. "In the Evening"

6. True or False: Plant wrote "All My Love" for his deceased son.

7. Which two band members had far fewer writing credits than usual on *In Through the Out Door*?
   a. Bonham and Jones
   b. Bonham and Plant
   c. Bonham and Page
   d. Page and Jones

8. Page produced the album and did a very good job on most tracks. However, he says that on one song, he made the singing indecipherable. Which song has the problematic vocal mixing?
   a. "I'm Gonna Crawl"
   b. "South Bound Saurez"
   c. "In the Evening"
   d. "Carouselambra"

9. Which of these statements is true regarding the cover of *In Through the Out Door*?

a. It was released in a brown paper bag.

b. It had ten different cover variations.

c. The name of the band wasn't anywhere on the packaging.

d. All of the above.

10. True or False: Because it was the era of punk rock and the beginning of new wave, *In Through the Out Door* didn't reach #1 in the US.

11. Plant and Bonham were hesitant to tour again. However, Grant pressured them into a significant acid test in front of over a hundred thousand fans at what festival?

a. Glastonbury

b. Knebworth

c. Pinkpop

d. Roskilde

12. True or False: Bonham's death did not come out of the blue. He collapsed during a show in 1980.

13. True or False: Led Zeppelin broke up the day John Bonham died.

14. The band was set to launch its first North American tour since 1977. Where was the first show, scheduled for 17 October 1980, scheduled to take place?

    a. Montreal

    b. New York

    c. Chicago

    d. Dallas

15. The album *Coda* included eight unreleased tracks from throughout the band's career. Which song on the album was an outtake from the *Led Zeppelin III* sessions?

    a. "We're Gonna Groove"

    b. "Poor Tom"

    c. "Ozone Baby"

    d. "Darlene"

16. Which song from *Led Zeppelin I* appears on *Coda* in the form of a rehearsal outtake?
    a. "Communication Breakdown"
    b. "Dazed and Confused"
    c. "How Many More Times"
    d. "I Can't Quit You Baby"

17. In 2015, Led Zeppelin released a deluxe edition of *Coda*. It included an early version of which song from *Led Zeppelin IV*?
    a. "Stairway to Heaven"
    b. "When the Levee Breaks"
    c. "Black Dog"
    d. "Four Sticks"

18. The song "Travelling Riverside Blues" was recorded by Zeppelin in 1969 and has become a favorite on classic rock radio over the years. In what year was it first officially released?
    a. 1982
    b. 1990
    c. 1997

d. 2008

19. The band appeared at the famous Live Aid benefit concert. It was not an inspiring performance. Who was the drummer at that show?

    a. Phil Collins
    b. Don Henley
    c. Jason Bonham
    d. Carmine Appice

20. In 2007, Led Zeppelin reunited again with Bonzo's son, Jason Bonham, on drums to perform at the Ahmet Ertegun Tribute Concert. The demand was so great that it broke the Guinness World Record for "Highest Demand for Tickets for One Music Concert." How many people tried to get a ticket?

    a. 1 million
    b. 2 million
    c. 4 million
    d. 20 million

ANSWERS

1. D- Oakland, California. The 1977 Led Zeppelin tour had seven shows left, but it had to be canceled after Plant's son died. Bonham died just after the band announced dates for a 1980 tour.

2. A- He had a fight with Grant's son. Grant's 11-year-old son, Warren, had gotten into a fight with the security guard. Then Graham and Bindon (who was a well-known thug in England) beat up the security guard. The concert had been organized by legendary promoter Bill Graham, who vowed he would never book Zeppelin again. A civil suit for $2 million was filed against the Zeppelin entourage.

3. B- Stockholm, Sweden. Led Zeppelin made a strange decision to record the album at Polar Studios, operated by pop group ABBA. The studio was brand new and had a ton of advanced equipment. Grant described the sessions as "a slog... It was cold and dark all the time."

4. C- Flew back to England. They recorded the album in winter when Stockholm is notably dark and depressing. However, there weren't too many of them since the album was done within three weeks.

5. A- "Fool in the Rain." The single reached #21 in the Billboard charts. It is a deceptively simple-sounding song. However, it has a tricky beat. The main section is in 12/8 meter, with an unusual polyrhythmic groove. Jones and Plant got the idea for the beat while watching the 1978 World Cup held in Argentina.

6. True. Plant said, "It was paying tribute to the joy that he gave us as a family." The song is often regarded as the best on the album. The song is also notable for mentioning the Welsh Goddess Arianrhod, who would lead the dead's souls to her castle located in the Aurora Borealis.

7. C- Bonham and Page. Bonham had no credits at all. Jimmy had only two when usually he was the primary writer for the songs. It has been suggested that Page contributed less because of his heroin problems. Cole says, "The truth of the matter was we never turned up until the middle of the night until we had scored. The other two got there when they were supposed to and just messed around doing stuff." However, Page contests that, "*In Through the Out Door* was done in a little over three weeks, so I couldn't have been in that bad shape. I'd never have been able to play, and I wouldn't have

been able to keep my head together to do this, that, and the other."

8. D- "Carouselambra." Plant said, "I thought parts of 'Carouselambra' were good, especially the darker dirges that Pagey developed." However, the sound of the vocals was frustrating. "I rue it so much now, because the lyrics on 'Carouselambra' were actually about that environment and that situation. The whole story of Led Zeppelin in its latter years is in that song, and I can't hear the words."

9. A- It was released in a brown paper bag. The cover actually had six variations, and you couldn't tell which one you got until the paper bag was removed. Designer Aubrey Powell remembers, "Peter said to me, 'We could put the album in a brown paper bag, and it would fucking sell. I said, 'Peter, what a great idea.' Atlantic didn't want the aggravation, but Peter said, 'We're fucking *doin'* it."

10. False. The album reached #1 on both sides of the Atlantic, as most Led Zeppelin albums did. The reaction was a positive surprise for the band. Plant remembers, "There was something going on, and it was lifting again. We decided that we could work, and we should start all over again."

11. B- Knebworth. The big festival was held annually to the north of London. Since the band had not played England since 1975, there was so much demand that they played an unprecedented second night. Plant does not remember the show fondly. "Knebworth was useless. It was no good because we weren't ready to do it, the whole thing was a management decision. It felt like I was cheating myself because I wasn't as relaxed as I could have been. There was so much expectation there, and the least we could have done was to have been confident enough to kill. We maimed the beast for life, but we didn't kill it. It was good, but only because everybody made it good. There was that sense of event."

12. True. Even though the band did not undertake any official tours that year, they had a series of low-key gigs in Europe. On 27 June in Nuremberg, Germany, Bonzo collapsed onstage. He was taken to a local hospital. Though there were rumors that drugs and alcohol were to blame, the band claimed he had overeaten.

13. False. The band officially broke up on 4 December 1980, a bit more than two months after the tragic death. Rumors swirled that they may replace Bonham. However, the band finally released a

statement reading, "We wish it to be known, that the loss of our dear friend and the deep respect we have for his family, together with the deep sense of undivided harmony felt by ourselves and our manager, have led us to decide that we could not continue as we were."

14. A- Montreal. The tour was called "THE 1980's PART ONE." It was supposed to end with four shows in Chicago in November.

15. B- "Poor Tom." It was yet another gem written by Page and Plant at the Bron-Yr-Aur cottage in Wales. "Poor Tom" is a character in Shakespeare's *King Lear*. Plant took the reference from John Steinbeck's classic novel *East of Eden*.

16. D- "I Can't Quit You Baby."

17. B- "When the Levee Breaks." The version was named "If It Keeps On Raining (When the Levee Breaks) (Rough Mix)."

18. B- 1990. The band was hesitant to release the song because it contained the "squeeze my lemon" bit, which was already released in "The Lemon Song" on *Led Zeppelin II*. However, the song is radically different from "The Lemon Song" and enjoys a good deal of popularity today. It was first included on the *Led Zeppelin Boxed Set*.

19. A- Phil Collins. Well, also session musician Paul Martinez. They played "Rock and Roll," "Whole Lotta Love," and "Stairway to Heaven." Collins remembers it as a terrible experience. "I didn't rehearse when I got there, but I listened to 'Stairway to Heaven' on Concorde. I arrived and went to the caravans, and Robert said: 'Jimmy Page is belligerent.'" He also remembered that "Robert wasn't match-fit. And if I could have walked off, I would have done, 'cause I wasn't needed, and I felt like a spare part." Robert admits his voice was a big part of the problem. "I'd done three gigs on the trot before I got to Live Aid. We rehearsed in the afternoon, and by the time I got on stage, my voice was long gone." Page called the performance "an atrocity."

20. D- 20 million. The band made tickets available online through a lottery system. They cost $250 each. This time the band was prepared and put on a good show. Jimmy said, "I knew it was going to sell out quickly, but the tidal wave of euphoria that preceded the gig—the anticipation—went beyond what I could possibly have imagined. We'd had a few shambolic appearances in the past, like Live Aid, so if we were ever going to come back together,

we were going to do it properly and stand up and be counted."

DID YOU KNOW?

- The writing and recording of *In Through the Out Door* saw the emergence of a new writing alliance within the band, Jones, and Plant. Jones says, "Robert and I were getting a bit closer — and probably splitting from the other two, in a way. We were always to be found over a pint somewhere, thinking, 'What are *we* doing?' And that went into *In Through the Out Door*. Basically, we wrote the album, just the two of us." Plant remembers it similarly: "Jonesy and I, who had never really gravitated toward each other at all, started to get on well. It was odd, but it gave the whole thing a different feel: things like 'All My Love' and 'I'm Gonna Crawl.' We weren't going to make another 'Communication Breakdown,' but I thought 'In the Evening' was really good." Grant nodded, saying, "John Paul Jones certainly did pick up the reins of the band with the *In Through the Out Door* album. People tended to think of him as a bass player, but he went far, far beyond that."

- John Bonham was experiencing depression and severe dependency on alcohol in 1980. He had begun to take Motival (a cocktail of the antipsychotic fluphenazine and the tricyclic antidepressant nortriptyline) to combat his anxiety and depression. That may have contributed to his death by interacting poorly with the alcohol. As a result, he was unenthusiastic about returning to the United States for a tour in September. Many believe that this fear was behind the binge drinking that ultimately led to his death. Plant remembers: "On the very last day of his life, as we drove to the rehearsal, he was not quite as happy as he could be. He said, "I've had it with playing drums. Everybody plays better than me." We were driving in the car, and he pulled off the sun visor and threw it out the window as he was talking. He said, 'I'll tell you what, when we get to the rehearsal, you play the drums, and I'll sing.' And that was our last rehearsal."

- Bonham died after an alarming drinking binge. It had lasted 12 hours. Over that time, he had consumed over 40 units of vodka. Jones found him in the morning. "Benje and I found him. It was like, 'Let's go up and look at Bonzo, see how he is.' We tried to wake him up... It was terrible. Then I had to tell the other two... I had to break the news to Jimmy and Robert. It made me feel very angry—at the waste of him... I can't say he was in good shape because he wasn't. There were some good moments during the last rehearsals...but then he started on the vodka...I think he had been drinking because there were some problems in his personal life. But he died because of an accident. He was lying down the wrong way, which could have happened to anybody who drank a lot." He had unfortunately choked on his own vomit. The police investigated but found no evidence of either foul play or that Bonham had suicidal intent.

- Though *In Through the Out Door* was not the band's finest moment, they felt that they had a great future ahead of them. Jimmy said, "Bonzo and I had already started discussing plans for a hard-driving rock album after that. We both felt that *In Through the Out Door* was a little soft... In its place, it was fine, but I wouldn't have wanted to pursue that direction in the future." Jones says that after Knebworth, he was very optimistic. "I think it was a special occasion for the band. But I'd have to say that I do look back on it with some sadness because it was really the start of a whole new era for us that never actually got going."

- Jimmy insists that the remastered versions of the classic Led Zeppelin albums, released in 2015, sound far superior to the original releases. He says, "What happens is, with these albums [is] that you find that the first test pressings are pretty good, but once they get them on the production line, then the quality, sort of, it starts to disappear a bit—or lack. With all of the advances of technology, that has sort of preceded the point that we can... that I can revisit the albums and re-cut them; then it gave the opportunity to give the best possible quality at this point. And really, actually—by hi-fi standards, this in, like reviews in hi-fi magazines—[they say] they're better than what the original ones were; which of course, that's always the object of the exercise." However, Jimmy was loyal to the original sound. "I'm not into re-writing history, I'm just re-presenting.

All of the music that you hear across the companion disc is all basically mixes from the time. I thought it was essential to have mixes from the time, because you've got the mindset, it's showing the mindset of what's being done. To go to the multi-tracks and start remixing, then that's a whole different total ballgame. I wasn't into that. I really wanted something whereby totally reflected what was going on at that point of time—of the time capsule, if you like, of when these things are being recorded. That's what the idea was of this."

CHAPTER VII:
PERSONAL LIVES AND BEHIND THE SCENES

1. At what age did John Bonham meet his future wife, Pat Phillips?

   a. 9

   b. 16

   c. 19

   d. 23

2. Robert had three children with Maureen Plant. Which one of these is not the name of one of their progeny.

   a. Carmen Jane

   b. Karac Pendragon

   c. Logan Romero

   d. Ashen Josan

3. The band bought a private plane that had belonged to a teen idol. How much had the previous owners spent to turn it into a flying rock 'n' roll dream?

a. $100,000

b. $200,000

c. $500,000

d. $1,000,000

4. Manager Peter Grant's drug problems were part of what began the dark chapter for the band in the late 70s. What triggered his severe dependency?

a. His back problems

b. His divorce

c. His financial problems

d. A death in the family

5. True or False: Before he worked as a manager, Peter Grant had been a professional wrestler.

6. Perhaps the most famous groupie story in rock history is known as "the mudshark incident." In what city did it occur?

a. Seattle, WA

b. Tampa, FL

c. Los Angeles, CA

d. Newport, RI

7. LA groupie Lori Maddox was underage when she met Jimmy Page and began their affair. How old was she?
   a. 14
   b. 15
   c. 16
   d. 17

8. On May 7, 1973, Led Zeppelin broke The Beatle's record for the largest crowd at a concert for a single group. Where were they playing?
   a. Tampa, Florida
   b. Miami, Florida
   c. Orlando, Florida
   d. Jacksonville, Florida

9. True or False: Robert had a child with the sister of his ex-wife Maureen.

10. Charlotte Martin was Jimmy's long-time girlfriend. Which guitarist did she date earlier in life?
    a. Jimi Hendrix

b. Eric Clapton

c. Keith Richards

d. George Harrison

11. True or False: Jimmy and Charlotte's daughter was conceived at the Bron-Yr-Aur cottage.

12. True or False: Jimmy went to jail after his second arrest for possession of cocaine in 1984.

13. True or False: Jimmy introduced Jason Bonham to cocaine when the latter was only 16 years old.

14. From 1980 to 2004, Jimmy owned a home in Windsor, which had previously belonged to a well-known English actor. Who was the actor?

a. Alec Guinness

b. Michael Caine

c. John Gielgud

d. Bob Hoskins

15. It has been rumored that the inspiration for Robert's love song "29 Palms" is a much younger singer. Who is the singer?
    a. Tori Amos
    b. P.J. Harvey
    c. Alannah Myles
    d. Liz Phair

16. True or False: John Paul Jones impregnated a Norwegian model in 1991 yet remained married to his long-time wife.

17. True or False: Jimmy is the wealthiest member of Led Zeppelin.

18. True or False: John Paul Jones turned down Jimmy and Robert's offer to join them for the *Unledded* reunion and tour.

19. During a Scandinavian tour, the band was sued by descendants of Count Zeppelin, the inventor of the Zeppelin. Therefore, they were briefly forced to change their name. What name did they adopt?
    a. The Nobs

b. The Pantaloons

c. The Jiminy Crickets

d. The Washing Machines

20. When Jimmy was 13, he appeared on British TV. He was asked what he wanted to do when he grew up. What did little Jimmy answer?

a. Be a musician

b. Cure cancer

c. Be an astronaut

d. Be a farmer

ANSWERS

1. B- 16. He met her when he was a young drummer at a show in Kidderminster. Not long after that, she was pregnant with their first child (the fantastic drummer Jason Bonham). It was a happy marriage. John's brother Michael says, "His love for her didn't diminish at all, through all their years together. Pat went with him everywhere."

2. D- Ashen Josan. That is the name of one of Jimmy's children.

3. B- $200,000. The band's first plane was cramped and uncomfortable. Therefore, they bought a former United Airlines Boeing 720B, which had belonged to teen idol Bobby Sherman. His manager, Ward Sylvester, turned the 138-seat passenger jet into what road manager Richard Cole called "a fucking flying gin palace." The amenities included a couch that ran the length of the plane, a fully-loaded bar with an electric organ, a video player stocked with everything from Marx Brothers' comedies to the latest porn, a separate drawing room with a faux fireplace, and a private master suite with a shower and a waterbed made of white

fur. The plane was later rented by Elton John, the Allman Brothers, the Rolling Stones, and Deep Purple.

4. B- His divorce. By all accounts, Grant was never the same after his marriage to former dancer Gloria fell apart. He left his wife along too often when on tour with the band, and it took its toll. He recalled, "I had some problems in 1975, and my wife was fed up with it all and walked out on me. It was not a good scene. There were drug problems with one or two people, including myself. It was really hard for me because I had to leave the kids, and my divorce was starting."

5. True. Peter was a bouncer at a bar owned by professional wrestler Paul Lincoln. Lincoln had the idea to be him in the ring. He helped Grant appear on television as a wrestler under the titles "Count Massimo" and "Count Bruno Alassio of Milan." Grant was massive, standing 6'2' tall and weighing over 300 pounds, and would often hit opponents with his belly. He also appeared in several movies, including *A Night to Remember* and *Cleopatra*.

6. A- Seattle, WA. If you are sensitive or queasy, do not read on! In 1969, the band stayed at the famous Edgewater Inn. One of the main attractions at that

hotel is that you can fish from the hotel room's window. Led Zeppelin was staying there with the American band Vanilla Fudge. According to a widely circulated story, a fish that was caught in the Pacific Ocean was then used on the most private parts of a young lady staying with the bands. Frank Zappa decided to write a song about it, which can be heard on his 1971 live album *Fillmore East*. Apparently, the story is accurate, and the episode was filmed in its entirety. However, most of the band was not involved. Only Bonham and road manager Richard Cole were, um, intimately involved.

7. A- 14. However, everyone mistook her for an older woman due to her mature look. Jimmy Page was infatuated with her and asked a roadie to bring her to his room at the Hyatt House in Los Angeles. When she arrived in the room, Maddox says the guitarist was wearing nothing but a hat over his eyes and was holding a cane. "He looked just like a gangster. It was magnificent." Their relationship was serious and went on for years.

8. A- Tampa, FL. Reportedly, attendance in Tampa was 56,800, with a $309,000 gross. They performed without an opening act or intermission for over

three hours. So the attraction was Led Zeppelin and only Led Zeppelin. Robert told a local newspaper, "I think it was the biggest thrill I've had. I pretend — I kid myself — I'm not very nervous in a situation like that. I try to bounce around just like normal. But, if you do a proportionate thing, it would be like half of England's population. It was a real surprise. Tampa is the last place I would expect to see 60,000 people. It's not the country's biggest city. It was fantastic. One would think it would be very hard to communicate; with 60,000 people, some have got to be quite a distance off. There were no movie screens showing us, like in Atlanta. The only thing they could pick on was the complete vibe of what music was being done."

9. True. Maureen and Robert divorced in 1983. He dated his ex-wife's sister Shirley for a while and had a son, Jesse Lee, in 1991.

10. B- Eric Clapton. After living with Eric Clapton, the French model had an affair with George Harrison. The Cream guitarist famously got his revenge when he broke up Harrison's marriage with English model Pattie Boyd. Eric recalls, "The reason why I deprived him [George] of the wife [Pattie] is that he

had put out his hand to my girl [Charlotte] first. I thought that I revenged it on him."

11. True. Plant said during Page and Plant's *Unledded* reunion in 1994 that Page's daughter, Scarlet, was conceived "about half an hour" after "That's the Way" was written.

12. False. Jimmy was indeed arrested twice for cocaine possession. Once in 1982 and again in 1984. However, he avoided going to jail.

13. True. Unfortunately, Jason remembers, "We got called to his room... I was 16 at this point, and there was a woman on the floor with a collar on, meowing, and he had this grinder thing...and he turned it over, and he went, 'Here you go,' and I went, 'Thanks.' He's like, 'You've done this before, right?' And I'm like, 'Yeah, of course, I have.' So he handed it over, and I just did all of it, and he went, 'Just like your father—you know, that was supposed to be for all of us.'"

14. B- Michael Caine. That was the home where Bonham was staying when he passed away.

15. C- Alannah Myles. The Canadian singer is best remembered for her hit "Black Velvet." Robert has never confirmed their affair. However, Myles has. She said she encouraged him not to seek a reunion

with Led Zeppelin. "I was trying to assist my lover, my man...with the decision." As for how they broke up: "It wasn't business that ended it...I don't know why. I went to America instead of going to England and marrying him. I sacrificed my love life for my recording career. We tried to stay in touch...it didn't work out."

16. False. Jones has been married to his wife Maureen since 1967. Their marriage has overcome all of the temptations and pitfalls of rock star marriage. Good for them.

17. False. Robert's net worth is said to be about $20 million. Robert is worth $200 million, and Jimmy is worth $180 million. John Paul Jones is worth $90, and Bonham was worth around $10 million when he passed away.

18. False. They didn't invite Jones, and he was very upset about it. He remembers, "I wasn't particularly glad for anybody at that point." Years later, it was still a point of contention, and Jones said that when he talks to Page, "we don't actually joke about it. It was quite a hard time for me. But we're past it if you know what I mean."

19. A- The Nobs. Understandably, they never adopted that name again.

20. C- Cure cancer. It looks like Jimmy still has something to aspire to.

DID YOU KNOW

- On 26 July 1977, Robert Plant's five-year-old son passed away due to a stomach virus. The singer was in New Orleans on tour at the time. Tour manager Richard Cole remembers, "the first phone call said his son was sick," describing a fateful pair of calls from Plant's wife. "And the second phone call, unfortunately, Karac had died in that time." Understandably, Robert lost interest in the band. He said, "I lost my boy. I didn't want to be in Led Zeppelin. I wanted to be with my family." He also stopped taking drugs. "I stopped taking everything on the same day," Plant added. "The most important thing to me is my family, and when I got off my face, I found it difficult to be all things to the people that meant a lot to me." As he later explained, "In '77, when I lost my boy, I didn't really want to go swinging around. 'Hey hey mama, say the way you move' didn't really have a great deal of import anymore."

- The band had a serious falling out over the death of Karac. Robert recalls that "during the absolute darkest times of my life when I lost my boy, and my family was in disarray, it was Bonzo who came to me. The other guys were [from] the South [of England] and didn't have the same type of social etiquette that we have up here in the North that could actually bridge that uncomfortable chasm with all the sensitivities required...to console." For reasons that are still not completely clear, Page and Jones did not come to the funeral. That did nothing to improve relations within the band.

- As we have seen, Jimmy had some serious struggles with drugs over the years. However, he has gotten clean. In his fifties, he stopped drinking and explained, "I don't drink alcohol," Page replied. "I think that makes quite a difference because it got to the point where I was in my fifties, and I thought I'm probably...I've got a good shot at getting to my seventies here."

- Many hard rock and metal bands are rumored to be into the occult. In the case of Jimmy Page, it is entirely true and was close to an obsession at one point. In particular, he was interested in the life and work of English occultist Aleister Crowley. Jimmy said, "I feel Aleister Crowley is a misunderstood genius of the 20th century. It is because his whole thing was liberation of the person, of the entity, and that restrictions would foul you up, lead to frustration, which leads to violence, crime, mental breakdown, depending on what sort of makeup you have underneath. The further this age we're in now gets into technology and alienation, a lot of the points he's made seem to manifest themselves all down the line." Page owned an occult bookstore and bought a home that belonged to Crowley. However, in his older years, he lost interest and sold both.

So ends our Led Zeppelin trivia extravaganza. We hope that you learned something about this legendary band. Now go put on some Zeppelin.

Made in United States
North Haven, CT
06 December 2021

11899372R10078